Deface the Currency

Samuel Alexander

DEFACE THE CURRENCY: THE LOST DIALOGUES OF DIOGENES

Published by the Simplicity Institute, Melbourne, 2016

www.simplicityinstitute.org

Copyright © 2016 Samuel Alexander

All rights reserved.

Cover by Andrew Doodson © 2016

Background image on cover is 'The School of Athens' by Raphael (1483-1520)

ISBN-13: 978-0-9941606-2-1

No part of this work may be reproduced, recorded, or transmitted in any form, whether in print or electronically, without the express written permission of the copyright owner.

Advance praise for *Deface the Currency*:

"This is a creative re-enactment of the life, death and ideas of the most influential Cynic of antiquity, Diogenes of Sinope. Lost after 2500 years, the dialogues attributed to him are here recovered through informed historical re-imagination, and in a series of six 'acts' Alexander takes his protagonist from his marketplace teachings through to the final condemnation of his works, and execution of his person. In this quasi-Socratic tragedy, Diogenes' ideas of simplicity, moderation and natural living are too revolutionary for an oligarchical system to tolerate, and yet prove too resilient to be permanently silenced. Alexander is faithful to the spirit of ancient authors and deftly works in subtle allusions to ancient sources – yet writes ever with an eye to present problems. His Diogenes becomes an essential voice for the revolutionary and potentially apocalyptic transitions of our own time."

– William Desmond, author of *The Greek Praise of Poverty*

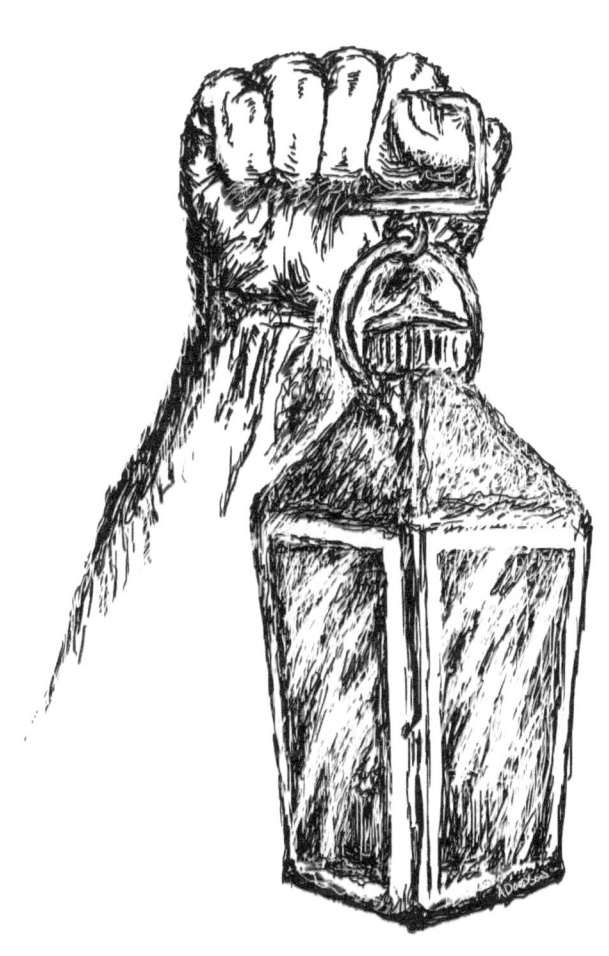

CONTENTS

Acknowledgements   ix
Preface   xi

ACT I   DIOGENES' LANTERN   1

ACT II   THE EMPEROR AND THE BEGGAR   13

ACT III   PLATO AND THE REPUBLIC OF DIOGENES   25

ACT IV   THE NERVOUS OLIGARCHS   41

ACT V   THE RENEGADE   49

ACT VI   DIOGENES IN PRISON   63

Acknowledgements

In an age of ecocide, spiritual malaise, and lost causes, what the world needs more than anything else are brave and joyful souls like Diogenes of Sinope – simple living pioneers who are prepared to swim against the tide of consumer culture and explore alternative conceptions of the good life, showing that with a little courage, boldness, and creativity it is possible to thrive in material simplicity.

This philosophical play, *Deface the Currency*, is dedicated to all those who challenge me to live more simply – Diogenes, Henry Thoreau, Ted, David and Su, Liam, Rachel and the other Wurruk'anians, Helen, the Agari mob, Adam and Annie, and all the frugal hedonists who are pioneering new pathways in the cultural landscape. May we create the taste by which we will be judged, and together build a new world within the shell of the old.

I feel very lucky to have friends who believe in my writing projects and are prepared to help bring them to fruition. In particular, I am much indebted to my editor, Antoinette Wilson, for combing through this text and removing the knots. Many thanks also to Andrew Doodson, for continuing to design my book covers with such flair. I must also acknowledge and thank Johnny Rutherford, Mark Burch, and Michael Green, for reading drafts of this text and helping me improve it.

As always, nothing I do would be possible without the love and support of my family and friends. Thank you for all the things that you do, large and small, which encourage me to keep on keeping on.

Preface

Diogenes of Sinope was a Greek philosopher, born in 412 BCE. His father, Hicesias, minted coins for a living, but when Diogenes was a young man both he and his father were embroiled in a scandal and exiled from Sinope for allegedly striking the face off coins. They lost their citizenship and all their possessions, thus initiating Diogenes' philosophical career as a wandering beggar.

Lore has it that upon being exiled Diogenes travelled to consult the Oracle at Delphi about how to live, and he received the reply: *paracharattein to nomisma*, a riddle typically translated as 'deface the currency'. Diogenes interpreted this advice to mean, not that he should deface coins, as such, but that he should deface the 'coin of custom', that is, he should expose the folly, vanity, and greed of human conventions and thereby change what people value. In particular, he set out to change the value of money, by showing that it was far less important to the good life and the good society than most people thought.

In that spirit, Diogenes lived a life of staggering material renunciation – a life of voluntary poverty. He embraced such a life in order to show himself and others that a full and flourishing life does not depend on material riches. He slept in a large ceramic barrel – often called a tub – dressed in rags, and possessed only a cup, a staff, and a lantern. He was always 'barking' at his contemporaries for living stupid, greedy, unfree lives, for which he earned the title 'the dog'. Despite his provocative eccentricities, by the time Diogenes died in 323 BCE he was recognised in Athens and beyond as a great philosopher, in an age of great philosophers.

It is thought that Diogenes wrote as many as thirteen dialogues, seven tragedies, a set of letters, and some poetry, although by all accounts none of his writings survive. Diogenes may also have written a political treatise called *The Republic* – a common title at the time – which described an anarchist utopia founded upon a culture and economy of 'simple living' and a politics of 'self-governance'. Some say that late in his life, at the request of a young friend, he also wrote or dictated a short summary of his philosophy, in the form of six dialogues, collectively entitled *Deface the Currency*.

Why is it that today none of Diogenes' writings survive, despite vast literatures from his philosophical contemporaries having survived? Was his vision of a 'simple living' utopia so threatening to the vested interests of the time that his books and essays were destroyed? And how is it that almost two and a half millennia after Diogenes died – in an age that needs his ideas more than ever – the present volume of Diogenes' dialogues have come to light? The answers lie within.

One final note before letting the text speak for itself. Although the following dialogues are set in ancient Athens, one could just as easily imagine them taking place in our own time, with Diogenes being recast as a dumpster-diving homeless man who haunts the shopping malls, and who engages the city Mayor rather than Alexander the Great and a distinguished university professor rather than Plato, and so forth. But whether the protagonist is ancient or postmodern, it is a testament to the depth of Diogenes' insight into the human situation that his ideas and ways of living can remain so relevant despite the gulf of time that separates us.

ACT I

Diogenes' Lantern

Athens, 323 BCE. In broad daylight Diogenes wanders barefoot through the marketplace, dressed in rags, with a burning lantern in one hand and a staff in the other. He holds the lantern out before him as if searching for something, although he is walking backwards. The merchants know that they are being mocked in some way but do not understand the meaning of Diogenes' provocation. They shake their heads in contempt and turn back to their petty business. A boy sits under a plum tree watching the scene with intrigue, trying to understand it. Eventually, as Diogenes drifts nearby, the boy plucks up the courage to engage the wandering beggar.

Boy [B]: Excuse me, sir.

Diogenes assumes it is not he who is being addressed.

B [louder]**:** Excuse me, sir, are you Diogenes the Dog?

Diogenes turns towards the boy and, now walking forwards, slowly approaches him with the lantern still outstretched. With faces close together, they stare at each other intensely until suddenly Diogenes barks loudly in the boy's face. The boy jumps back in fright, shielding himself from an attack. After a moment the boy drops his guard.

B: So it is you.

Diogenes shrugs his shoulders and turns away, resuming his search, again walking backwards.

B: You know they call you 'Socrates gone mad', don't you, Diogenes?

Diogenes again turns towards the boy and, walking forwards, slowly moves closer. They stare into each other's eyes for a time but once more Diogenes merely barks loudly. The boy doesn't flinch. Diogenes shrugs again and walks away, backwards.

B [after a pause]: You certainly seem mad, Diogenes. Barking mad. As for being Socratic – well, that's not so clear.

Diogenes stops and turns to look at the boy from a distance.

Diogenes [D]: Tell me this, boy, you who are so quick to accuse me of insanity: what good is it to appear sane in an insane world? Our civilisation is sick to the core! So be very suspicious, I say, of anyone who appears well adjusted to the sickness, for they can only be sick themselves. I would rather not pretend, you see, and to instead live truthfully in this false world. I counsel you to do the same. The crazier the world is, the crazier sanity will look. Isn't that so?

B: I cannot fault your logic, Diogenes.

D: Everyone – and by that I mean *everyone* – is within a finger's breadth of insanity. For instance, if a man raises his first finger and speaks, people think him wise. If he raises his middle finger, they think him mad. It is merely my job to show people the middle way.

Diogenes howls like a dog while raising his middle finger to the merchants, then resumes his search, chuckling to himself, again walking backwards.

B: Don't go, Diogenes. Some say you are the keeper of truth, and all I know is that I know not. Tell me, how is one to live in times like these? What should I do with my life? Like the merchants over there, I'm lost – only I know it.

As if in response to the question, Diogenes plucks a plum from the tree and begins to eat it. As he does so, he sweeps his rags to one side, crouches, and defecates unashamedly under the plum tree. There are cries of disgust from the marketplace.

D: I hope you appreciate the point of my philosophical vulgarity, young man, which is not gratuitous, though it appears to be lost on these vulgar merchants. Nourish that which nourishes you, boy, and live in accordance with nature. That is all you need to know. Now kindly leave me alone, I am looking for something.

Diogenes spits his plum stone into his waste, kicks some soil over it, then raises his lantern to resume his search, walking backwards.

B: But, Diogenes...

Diogenes interrupts with a bark, then pauses, as if checking his message was received. Eventually, he continues on his way. The persistent boy follows.

B: You can bark all you like, Diogenes the Dog. You can even bite me or strike me with your staff. But no matter how hard you bite or strike, I will remain willing to listen and stand at your side, like a faithful hound, so long as you speak the truth.

On hearing this Diogenes pauses for a moment and eventually turns around.

D: It should worry you, boy, that you sound a lot like me as a younger man, pleading with Antisthenes to take me on as a student. It takes a brave and stubborn soul to follow the dogs, boy. You are either incredibly wise or incredibly stupid. We'll find out soon enough, I suppose. Come, let us sit a while, these old legs are weary from the search.

They sit. After a while the boy opens his mouth to speak, but Diogenes raises his hand in objection. They sit for a while in silence [long pause].

D: You have received your first lesson. Please reiterate for me the essential message.

Perplexed, the boy ponders the meaning of Diogenes' lesson. Unexpectedly, as he sits quietly next to Diogenes, the boy becomes enraptured by the soft breeze on his face in the morning sun. In the goodness of time he proceeds to offer an answer.

B: Diogenes, you have shown me the unceasing eloquence of silence. I can only assume your message is that the beauty of ordinary existence can be ruined by adding unnecessarily to it, and that perhaps we already have everything we need to flourish and prosper, provided we look at life the right way and act accordingly. For a moment, just then, as the soft breeze was touching my face in the morning sun, I swear I was the richest man in the world, richer than Alexander the Great. But that sounds silly when I say it.

Diogenes listens intently and raises his lantern to the boy's face once more.

D: It is my pleasure and honour to meet you, young brother. This dog is no master, nor does he seek one beyond Truth and Nature, but if you can tolerate my company, I can tolerate yours. It takes a wise man to discover a wise man. I am Diogenes of Sinope, at your service.

B: I am Philiscus of Aegina, son of Onesicritus.

They shake hands.

D: And why, Philiscus, was I walking backwards just now?

B: Well, one can never be sure with you, Diogenes. I heard the merchants mocking you for doing so. But I feel that they should be ashamed, for they walk backwards along the whole path of existence, and laugh at you for merely walking backwards along the path of the promenade. Does that answer suffice?

D: Yes, indeed, Philiscus, you understand things well enough.

They sit together for a time in silence.

D: Were you going to eat that weed over there, my friend?

B: No, Diogenes, I was not.

D: Do you mind if I do?

B: Why, no, Diogenes, not at all – although you are aware, no doubt, that eating in the marketplace is frowned upon.

Diogenes reaches over and pulls a weed from the earth and begins to chew on it.

D: If it is in the marketplace where my belly rumbled, why not eat here? Bah! The customs and conventions of this world are strange, indeed. Acting in accordance with nature – frowned upon though it is – is certainly preferable to being invited to the dinner parties of the rich, for then I must eat when they are hungry, and that makes no more sense than putting on clothes when the rich are cold.

B: From what I can tell, Diogenes, the rich are hungry no matter how much they eat; cold, no matter how many clothes they have; and yet, here I see you, fit, strong, and healthy, despite being of considerable age, feasting on weeds and dressed in rags, with an eternal smile on your face.

D: He who has the most is most content with the least.

B: You speak the truth, Diogenes – although I am taught the opposite in school. But people laugh at you for saying such things, you know?

D: Well, so do the asses laugh at them. But just as they do not care for the asses laughing at them, neither do I care for the asses laughing at me. I assure you, at the end of their lives, if not before, those merchants over there will go home, look at themselves in the mirror, and see only an ass staring back. Then their laughter will come back to haunt them, for they will realise that they have lived a fool's life.

B: I do not want to live a fool's life, Diogenes.

The boy reaches over, pulls out a weed, and raises it to his mouth.

D: I wouldn't eat that one, my friend; it will kill you. That's hemlock.

Diogenes reaches over, pulls out a weed from a different patch, and passes it to the boy, who examines it, throwing the hemlock away.

B: This simple life you practise isn't very simple, Diogenes. Some might even say that it is dangerous. It might even get you killed!

The boy eats the weed Diogenes gave him, nodding approvingly.

B: But it holds unexpected delights.

D: These are the paradoxes, my boy, that flow from believing contradictory truths such as 'less is more'.

Diogenes draws < = > in the sand with his staff.

D: Beat that Pythagoras! Beyond your theorem, here lies Diogenes' Praxis! This is why I am so happy and carefree, my friend, even if, admittedly, I am also irritated easily and increasingly cantankerous in the presence of fools.

B: You certainly don't seem to care much if people laugh at you, Diogenes. Only yesterday I saw you begging for money from a statue! Would you care to explain that to me? I might have even laughed at you myself.

D: Begging from statues gets me used to being refused, young brother. Only then do I feel ready to try my luck with people.

B: And the result?

D: I have lost a lot of weight but gained a philosophy!

Diogenes laughs.

B: Why is it, Diogenes, that people will give alms to the blind and crippled, but never to philosophers?

D: Because, young man, people know that one day they could be blind or crippled, but they never dream they will take up philosophy.

Diogenes laughs again.

B: I am surprised you haven't starved to death, Diogenes. How do you survive?

D: Nature provides well enough for creative souls with simple needs, my friend. And when necessary, I steal from the temples.

B: What! That is an unusual practice for a philosopher who preaches about how to live an ethical life.

D: Not at all, just think about it. Everyone knows that the gods are friends of the wise, and friends are a community who share their goods. Since I am a wise man, I know that the gods want to share their goods with me. How's that for philosophy?

B: I'll need to think further on that, Diogenes. Do you really believe in the gods?

D: How can I not? Just look at all of the god-forsaken people around here! If the gods do not exist, they ought to exist, if only to ensure these people have a hell to go to when they die. People go to the temples and pray for their health, only to return home and feast until they are sick!

B: Would they sooner find what they seek by adopting your simpler ways?

D: Undoubtedly that is the case. The gods provide all people with the means to be happy, young brother, yet people devote their lives to making themselves and others miserable. And they call me mad.

Diogenes sighs deeply.

B: Despite the wisdom of your words, Diogenes, it is hardly surprising they call you mad. After all, I just saw you wandering through the marketplace, in broad daylight, with a burning lantern! I can understand why you eat weeds, walk backwards, and beg from statues, but I can't for the life of me understand why you carry around a lantern in the daytime.

D: Do you really want to know, young brother?

B: I do, Diogenes.

D: Are you prepared to be blinded by the light?

B: If that is what it will take, Diogenes, I am sure my eyes will eventually adjust.

D: Well then, if you think you are ready...

Diogenes pauses for a moment and his mood becomes more sullen and serious. He turns to look the boy in the eye.

D: I carry my burning lantern, my friend, because of the terrible darkness that envelops us. The sun has almost set on this civilisation of ours – the evening light is fading as we speak – and thus only with my lantern burning can I hope to find a community of honest men and women with whom to converse.

The boy looks around, confused.

B: You talk of darkness, Diogenes, but all I see is daylight. The sun is shining as brightly as ever. Perhaps in your old age your eyes are failing you?

D: I am afraid you are like the fish that does not know it is in water, failing to perceive the fabric of existence on account of it being omnipresent. Signs of descent are everywhere, young brother, and if you cannot see those signs then I am afraid it is your eyes that are failing, not mine. The bridge of civilisation has been crumbling for so long now, and so slowly, that people do not often notice its deterioration. But the pillars holding it up have been compromised so fundamentally that it risks collapsing at any moment. I used to sleep under that bridge over there, my friend, but wouldn't dare to do so these days. It's only a matter of time – whether it falls sooner or later, it doesn't really matter. Descent is inevitable: our task now is to descend with dignity.

B: If what you say is true, Diogenes – that the world is darker and more fragile than most people perceive – then it would follow that what the world needs more than anything else is enlightenment.

D: Exactly so! Nothing is more important than a new consciousness, my boy, for we are living in a society made up of slaves who think that they are free and free spirits who think they are slaves. If our minds are not in order, all else is lost. We are freer than we think we are. That is why the Oracle at Delphi ordered me to deface the currency.

B: Deface the currency? I have heard, of course, that you and your father debased the coinage many years ago and for that you were both exiled from Sinope. But I had thought all that was behind you now. Are you telling me that you are still defacing the currency?

D: Why, it is my life's work! The Oracle did not intend for me to continue defacing actual coins but to deface the coin of custom, the 'currency' of our times. And since it is customary to think that money is the most important thing in the world, I have taken it upon myself to change the value of money, to expose the errors of conventional economic valuation. Thus I deface the currency.

B: I think I am beginning to understand you, Diogenes. When you masturbate in public, for example, it is only to make the point that people do that every day by living such vain, materialistic lives. You do not do this to pleasure yourself but to provoke others to consider their own shamelessness.

D: At last, I am understood! I was beginning to worry that posterity would only remember me as some shameless old pervert! Hopefully one day I can put the false coin out of circulation.

B: One thing, however, is not clear to me, Diogenes. What were you searching for so intently, with your lantern?

D: I was in search of a just and honest person, young brother, and in this overcrowded marketplace I had only found rascals and scoundrels, until I found myself talking with you, a man among boys.

The two friends sit for a moment in silence.

B: I have learnt much from you already, Diogenes. For now, however, I had better get home.

D: Well, just remember that teaching is a two-way street. I expect you to teach me things too.

B: Never could I hope to teach anything to a man as wise as you, Diogenes. But I will forever be your humble student. Goodbye for now.

The boy runs off, stopping to drink from the river with his cupped hands. Diogenes looks at his cup, then throws it away in disgust.

D: What! A child has beaten me in plainness of living! Fool that I am, to have been carrying superfluous baggage all this time!

ACT II

THE EMPEROR AND THE BEGGAR

Diogenes is basking in the sun near his tub. Alexander the Great enters the scene with two imperial guards. After motioning to the guards to remain at a distance, the Emperor approaches the sleeping beggar, examining the unusual scene with interest. Eventually Alexander clears his throat to announce his arrival. Diogenes does not stir. The Emperor clears his throat again, this time more loudly. Diogenes opens one eye, assesses the situation, then returns to sleep. Alexander does not retreat.

Alexander [A]: Tell me, great Diogenes, if you are the wise philosopher they say you are, why are you known as 'the dog'?

After a time Diogenes again opens one eye and peers up at his visitor.

Diogenes [D]: They call me the dog because I protect my friends, bark at strangers, and bite greedy scoundrels – so I'd recommend you keep at a safe distance. I sleep under the stars or here in my kennel, I eat what I can find lying around, I obediently obey my masters, Truth and Nature – and I sleep when I am in boring company. Now, if you will excuse me.

Diogenes returns to his sleep. Alexander turns to his guards and questioningly holds out his hands, not used to being shown such indifference. Unperturbed, however, he again attempts to start a dialogue.

A: Allow me to introduce myself, Diogenes: I am your Emperor, Alexander the Great.

Diogenes sighs deeply and eventually sits up.

D: I know who you are, I just don't understand why you are still here when it is clear I am busy. You are not waiting for me to bow down before you and kiss your royal feet, are you? Only a few moments ago I was searching through that pile of bones over there, in search of the bones of your ancestors, and I could not distinguish them from the bones of your slaves. You are but a man, Alexander – your shit stinks too – so do not come here expecting me to treat you like an Emperor. There is only one ruler of men here, and it isn't you. Now, if you should like to kiss my paw, very well, but then be gone with you.

Diogenes holds up a foot, a gesture Alexander ignores.

A: Diogenes, I come here in good faith, on account of the stories I have been told of your great wisdom and insight. As you will no doubt be aware, I am the richest and most powerful man in the Empire…

Diogenes bursts out laughing.

A: … and I am here to offer you anything that you may want. Anything at all that you may need or desire, I am willing and able to provide. You look destitute, living here in this tub. Tell me, what can I do for you? Simply name your wish – anything at all – and I will humbly oblige.

D: All I want, great Alexander, is for you to stand out of my sunlight.

A: Excuse me? You can't be serious.

D: Unshadow me! If you will not leave me alone, at least grant me nature's warmth, which is all I need and something you cannot provide... only interfere with, it seems.

Alexander looks up towards the sun and back to Diogenes, then steps to the side, granting Diogenes his wish.

A: I have to say, Diogenes, you are quite the enigma.

D: Not so, Alexander. I am but a simple man with simple needs. Why is that so hard to understand? I just do not want what you boast of having; I just do not need what you think you can provide. It is the privilege of the gods to want nothing, and for godlike men and women to want little.

A: It appears so, Diogenes, and that is precisely why you are an enigma. Most people envy the rich and powerful, and you seem to offer nothing but disdain.

D: That's just the thing, Alexander: you are *not* rich and powerful. You are poor, burdened, sad, confused, weak, lonely, insecure, misguided, anxious, and lost... if only you knew it. But if you stick around long enough, my Emperor – and it seems you aren't leaving – then you are at risk of *becoming* rich and powerful.

Diogenes stands to look Alexander in the eye.

D: If it does not terrify you too much, I might even set you free.

There is a long silence as the two men gaze deeply into each other's eyes.

A: You, a beggar, might set me – Alexander the Great – free. Is that what you are saying?

D: The art of being a slave is to rule one's master.

A: I am intrigued, Diogenes, to say the least. By all means, set me free!

Alexander bows facetiously before Diogenes.

D: Are you sure?

A: I am sure.

D: Are you sure you are sure?

A: I am sure I am sure.

D: Are you sure you are sure you are sure?

A: Diogenes, this could go on for some time.

D: Very well, Alexander, sit down and pay attention, for I would rather be lying quietly in the sun.

The two men sit down next to each other.

D: Tell me, Alexander: what do you want from life? What are your grand plans?

A: That is a fair question, Diogenes, and a good place for a philosopher to start. My immediate plans are to finish conquering and subjugating Greece.

D: Then what?

A: Then I plan to conquer and subjugate Asia Minor, followed by North Africa. It is within my power, I can assure you.

D: Then what?

A: Well, Diogenes, I am a man of great ambition. Ultimately, I shall rule the entire world.

D: It seems to me that you are utterly lacking in ambition, but nevertheless. Suppose you achieve your goals in coming years, Alexander – these goals you call ambitious. Then what?

A: What do you mean, then what?

D: I mean what I said. Having conquered the entire world, then what? What will that allow you to do? Why would that be important and worthwhile?

A: By that stage, Diogenes, I will be so unimaginably rich and powerful that at last I will be able to relax and enjoy myself, to live a quiet life of leisure, meaningful work, and creativity, which is all I truly seek.

D: Perhaps you might even be able to bask in the sun as I was doing before you interrupted me?

A: Precisely, Diogenes. Having conquered the entire world, I should then be able to bask in the sun as you were just doing.

Diogenes looks at Alexander and shakes his head.

D: Why not save yourself and others a lot of trouble, Alexander, and bask in the sun with me now?

A: Diogenes, I cannot do that until I have conquered the world! Were you not listening?

D: But you just told me, you silly git, that what you truly seek is a quiet life in which you are able to relax and bask in the sun. It seems to me, therefore, that your plans to conquer the world are utterly misguided. First conquer yourself, as I have done, for then you will discover that conquering the world is but the infantile desire of a dim-witted child.

A: Excuse me?

D: Whom are you trying to impress with your grand plans, Alexander? Mummy and daddy? Ignore their expectations, I say – ignore everyone's expectations – and follow the path of Truth and Nature. Like every man and woman of our decadent and degraded times, you treat wealth and power as an end in itself, when really it is merely a means. Thus you are left wasting your life chasing the wrong things. If only you would keep a closer eye on the true end, you'd discover how few are the means required.

A: You make it sound like I am an archer aiming for the wrong target.

D: All I know is that if life were an archery competition I would happily stand right by the target, because only there would I feel safe. The archers of this world, aiming for the prizes of life, are incompetent fools, and you are the paragon, the prime example, puffed up by the conceit of a false wealth. It even looks like you are trying to use the arrow to shoot the bow, which gives the impression you are an imbecile. Everywhere I look I see people like you pursuing petty things by nasty means, and it invokes in me a mixture of sadness, laughter, and contempt.

A: But surely people are justified in seeking wealth and power in order to achieve their aims, in order to live a life of comfort?

D: It would be a sad creature who, at the end of life, could say only that they lived comfortably. To aim for comfort lacks ambition. Better one lives passionately and meaningfully in discomfort, than a life of comfortable unfreedom, as people seem content to do today. But of course, living well still depends on material conditions sufficient for a humble life of freedom – I would never deny that. It is just that conventionally people seek wealth and power *as* their aim, and thus they never stop pushing others down in order to get ahead. You see, most people in our culture are always waiting to live the good life *later* – and then they die. This is a terrible shame, because every moment is like a melting snowflake, perfect in its fleeting beauty if looked upon in the right way.

A: Hmmm. You certainly challenge the spirit of our times, Diogenes.

D: Well, please accept my challenge, Alexander. I suspect that you have a very distorted understanding of what wealth and power really are, which is what leads you and almost everyone else down the dead end of an acquisitive life. You seem to think of wealth in material terms and power in terms of authority over others. But, as I have implied, these are false, childish conceptions, befitting only greedy, narrow-minded, hare-brained dupes. After all, you just offered me anything I wanted and I could have asked for palaces and armies. But I told you there was nothing you had that I wanted or needed. Who, then, is richer? Who is more powerful? Who is freer? Is it you, Alexander, who has so much but still desperately wants more? Or is it Diogenes, who has so little but is perfectly content?

A: I am beginning to wonder whether it is you, Diogenes. But I have to say, you are turning my world upside down.

D: That was the most insightful thing you've said all day. There is hope for you yet!

Diogenes laughs.

A: You have been highly critical of me, Diogenes, and of all those who pursue material riches, fame, and worldly power. But a man cannot merely be a critic. What constructive alternative could you possibly provide?

D: My life is my message, Alexander. Self-taught, voluntary poverty is the path of the philosopher, for the things which philosophy attempts to teach by reasoning, poverty forces us to practise. Do you understand?

A: I think so, but perhaps you could explain things further, just so I am sure.

D: Certainly. One of the most complex questions we face when thinking about how we ought to live our lives is the question of material wealth: how much is enough? But it turns out that we cannot answer this question until we answer a prior question: enough for what? That prior question requires us to have a chief end in life, a goal, a purpose, which lies beyond material advancement. What is money *for,* Alexander? What is power *for*? It would be no good getting to the end of life surrounded by material riches, only to discover that nice cushions, fast chariots, and magnificent palaces simply cannot satisfy the human need for meaning and satisfaction.

A: I should not want to get to the end of my life and discover that I had not lived.

D: Well, then, you had better pay attention because you are well on your way to a wasted life, my Emperor. Indulge me for a moment: imagine you are lying on your deathbed this very moment. As you are about to pass on to the next world, what goals and attitudes would you want to have defined your life? Would you care much for fame and social status? Would you wish that you had spent more time coveting palaces or conquering territories?

A: I doubt it, Diogenes. I am sure I would wish that I had spent *less* time planning for military or financial expansion, which is a nasty business really, and more time basking in the sun, talking with friends, reading the most enriching books, listening to the most beautiful music, and otherwise engaging in peaceful, creative activity. I can't imagine that splendid houses or fine clothing – or even being ruler of a global Empire – will be of much comfort when I am on my deathbed. I am quite sure now that true contentment lies elsewhere, in a simpler, more humble way of life.

D: You are beginning to show real promise, my student. You are quite right to say that material riches or military conquests won't provide much satisfaction at the end of one's life, but I ask you to think about whether those things are even desirable right now. With all your material wealth, I should think that you are constantly worried that others may steal it from you or murder you for it.

A: That comes with being far richer than other people, Diogenes, and is a constant source of anxiety and distrust.

D: And I should think that there might be more noble things to do with one's life than oppress the people of this world and demand that they call you Emperor.

A [pause]**:** I suppose, if I look at things from their perspective, they would see me as a greedy tyrant.

D: Indeed, for that is precisely what you are! And I should think that in a world where great multitudes are dying of hunger and disease, claiming so many of the world's resources for yourself is rather perverse.

A: I suppose – now that you have forced me to reflect – I may have taken somewhat more than my fair share.

D: And I should think that the people you impress by being a greedy tyrant with nice clothes could only be scoundrels themselves, and that those who befriend you only do so for their own interests, and so can't be genuine friends. It follows that you are a friendless megalomaniac admired only by scoundrels or fools. Far from being rich and powerful, then, it would seem that you are terribly poor, weak, and, I have to say, a bit sad.

A: Need you go on, Diogenes! I think you have made your point well enough. I came here claiming to be the richest and most powerful man in the world, but you have demonstrated beyond question that my self-image is, or was, horribly flawed. I feel like I have just been led out of a dark cave and my eyes have yet to adjust to the light.

D: Brace yourself, Alexander, for when your eyes adjust you will find that the world is a dark place.

Alexander pauses in reflection.

A: If that is so, Diogenes, how is one to live? You seem to embrace life as a gift to be treasured; I should even call you happy. Are you saying that darkness and happiness can coexist?

D: One is not happy because of the darkness but in spite of it. Each human being is charged with the task of creating the meaning of their life in the world as it is, just as a sculptor must shape something worthy from a given lump of clay. Granted, we may not get to choose which lump of clay we start with in life, but we are free to shape what we are given into what we have the imagination to envision.

A: It sounds like you are saying that life is like art.

D: No, I am saying that life *is* art – it is our most important creative challenge. The great painter who is brilliant with the brush but who lives like a knave is not much of an artist in my eyes. He has misdirected his vital creativity: too much good painting at the expense of good living, which ultimately reflects poorly on the painting. And just as the artist, when at work, should paint the picture that expresses his most noble visions or intimate emotions, and not paint the picture desired by upper class fools, so must we, as free individuals, not shape our lives to conform to the expectations of idiots in an idiotic society, but instead shape something worthwhile.

A: Perhaps you are right, Diogenes, but how does this relate to your doctrine of simplicity?

D: That should be clear, I would have thought. The painter must avoid unnecessary brush strokes or else the painting will be no good. So too must we, in life, avoid unnecessary things or else we will be distracted from our proper pursuits and our existence will be no good. You are the perfect example of how not to live, I'm afraid to say. So busy are you pursuing unnecessary things – what you call wealth and power – that you have no time or energy for painting a worthy self-portrait. I see an ugly character forming, Alexander, ruined by superfluous brush strokes. Beauty lies in simplicity. Just look at the stars at night – such divine economy! Live simply and be free.

A [pause]**:** Just as you said you would, Diogenes, I am coming to think that your words have liberated me from myself.

D: You have, at least, begun the endless journey, Alexander. Now, perhaps, you will allow me to return to my luxurious existence basking here in the sun, for time is the most valuable thing one can spend, and I feel that I have spent enough of it with you for now.

A: Of course, great Diogenes. I cannot thank you enough. I remain a man of great ambition but my ambitions have suddenly transformed beyond recognition. I look upon the world with fresh eyes, as if I have just gained consciousness for the first time. May our paths cross again someday soon.

Alexander bows humbly before Diogenes and takes his leave. When he reaches his guards, he comments to them:

A: If I were not Alexander, I should wish to be Diogenes.

Diogenes overhears the comment and mumbles to himself:

D: If I were not Diogenes, I should also wish to be Diogenes.

ACT III

PLATO AND THE REPUBLIC OF DIOGENES

Early one morning Diogenes is washing lettuce, lentils, and grapes on the steps of Plato's Academy. Before long Plato arrives to prepare for the day's lectures and is greeted by Diogenes.

Diogenes [D]: Forgive my insanity of mood, Plato, but it's an exquisite day to be alive, is it not? Behold, the cosmos is humming warmly with good vibrations; the very fabric of existence is soft but exhilarating; even the air and light on this glorious morning seem to be carriers of a quiet virtue. And yet, you look out of balance, somehow; agitated and hurried. Is your mind in order, great philosopher? Perhaps you would care for a share of these grapes?

Plato stops to look at Diogenes suspiciously.

D: I have surplus. Would you care for a share?

Cautiously Plato accepts the grapes and proceeds to eat them all.

D: I said a *share* of those grapes, Plato! You've gone and eaten them all, you gluttonous wretch.

Plato [P]: Forgive me Diogenes, in circumstances of abundance it is very hard not to take more than one's rightful share. I am not thinking straight.

D: It would seem so, Plato. Clearly you are but a particular case of Universal Man – a featherless biped, you would say, with an appetite for excess. Ha! Quite a definition for our miserable species! Accurate enough, as far as it goes.

Diogenes holds out a plucked chicken and throws it at Plato's feet.

D: There is Platonic Man for you – a relation, perhaps?

P: You know, Diogenes, if you were prepared to pay respects to Dionysus you would not need to sit there washing lettuce and lentils.

D: Ah, great Plato, if you were prepared to eat lettuce and lentils you would not need to flatter Dionysus. Indeed, I should like to see you practise the moderation of which you preach a little more sincerely or else stay quiet on the subject altogether. Better still, close your Academy and stay quiet on all subjects! Now that would be a noble undertaking.

P: Thank you for your advice, Diogenes, but please excuse me if I ignore the words of a homeless beggar. The Academy is thriving, I am pleased to say. Perhaps you might like to join us today?

D: Funny you should say that, Plato, for I had intended to do just that. In fact, that is why I am here preparing my meal of lentils.

P: Oh, Diogenes, you know lentils just make a man gaseous. Must you really come to class only to let out hot air?

D: Why, Plato, I was just following your lead. In fact, I've been writing a tragedy in your honour.

P: Have you just – and what is it called?

D: *The Fart.*

P: Well, good luck with that, Diogenes. Perhaps you should think of doing some serious work one day. In the Academy today we will be discussing the nature of a Republic founded upon justice. Now, I must run along to prepare my lecture.

Plato turns to leave.

D: Please don't go so soon, Plato. I am wondering whether by way of preparation we could discuss the nature of a just Republic right now, on the steps of your Academy? It's a magnificent day for philosophising under the sun, wouldn't you agree? You see, I have been working on a political treatise of my own, called *The Republic*, and I believe my perspectives might assist in the clarification of your own thought. I'd be happy to sketch a picture of my utopia if you'd be prepared to listen. After all, you talk twice as much as you listen even though you have two ears and only one tongue. Listening more might do you some good. What do you say?

P: The Republic of Diogenes, aye? Ha! I had no idea you had a political bone in your body.

D: Excuse me! My life is nothing if not political, Plato. I am surprised you cannot see that. What could be more political than living one's values, spending one's time raising awareness about important issues, engaging with one's community, and trying to build the new world within the shell of the old? Compare this life of mine to the typical citizen of Athens, who votes once every few years, and otherwise drifts along with the times, like a stick in a river, thinking their political work is done. A true political actor must seek to direct the flow of the river in the most appropriate direction, in moments great and small, and not just go with the flow. Otherwise one is merely a pawn in a game one is not playing.

P: I suppose I had a rather narrow view of politics, Diogenes, as something that focused only on rulers and their rules. But if by politics we could also mean the governance or self-governance of a community or city-state, by the people themselves rather than by their representatives, then I suppose your way of life can be considered political too. Perhaps a discussion with you might bear fruit after all.

Plato sits down next to Diogenes.

D: Would you like a bowl of lentils to provide some sustenance?

P: If you wouldn't mind, that would be good. I didn't have time to eat this morning. Are you not having any?

D: No, Plato, I'm not hungry just now.

Diogenes hands a bowl of lentils to Plato, who begins to eat.

P: Where should we begin, then?

D: As philosophers, we should begin with Truth, surely? It is my view that a just government must be transparent and truthful at all times.

P: That seems like a good place to start.

D: Well, I am surprised to hear you agree, Plato, for your Republic notoriously is founded upon a 'Noble Lie' which attempts to artificially establish three classes of people: the commoners, the soldiers, and the guardians. I put it to you, my philosophical friend, that if a guardian wore the garb of a commoner, or vice versa, neither you nor I could not tell them apart. And I've certainly met common farmers who were infinitely wiser than politicians. So it seems your Noble Lie is certainly a lie, but 'noble', that I cannot accept. It seems arbitrary, and arbitrary rule is what I detest most in politics. Your Republic, I'm afraid, has a rotten core.

P: I do not accept it is rotten, Diogenes, but perhaps, on second thoughts, it was somewhat unphilosophical of me to found my Republic upon three classes that are not really grounded in nature.

D: Somewhat unphilosophical? It is an intellectual scandal for which your Academy should be shut down! Let me guess: you would be one of the guardians who hold all the political power.

P: It sounds self-serving, perhaps, but yes, my Republic is one where philosophers are kings, and kings, philosophers.

D: Hmmm. Would you let your students mark their own essays, Plato?

P: No, of course not, because they would have an incentive to be deceitful and place themselves at the top of the class, even if they didn't deserve it.

D: Well, so too with your Republic! Never trust a philosopher, I say, who tells the world that philosophers are a special class of humanity and that philosophers should be kings. And never trust politicians who claim they will serve our interests when we know they only serve their own. In my

Republic, Plato, every human being is expected and encouraged to live the examined life of a philosopher and the engaged life of a politician. Accordingly, there would be no need for the guardian class, for we would all be mature enough to govern ourselves. No better way to abolish the class of guardians, I say, than for us all to be guardians in common.

P [reflecting]: Guardians in common, you say. This Republic of yours sounds like it could have some merit, Diogenes, even if it is rather too utopian for my taste. But the very idea is expanding my imagination. You surprise me.

D: Well, you appal me, Plato. Worse than being unphilosophical, your Republic is unjust!

P [offended]: How so?!

D: Plato, there are no inherent differences between human beings of a kind that could justify a society based on class. So your Republic must be rejected as both unphilosophical and unjust. The only Republic that accords with reason is a classless society where each and every human being is treated as morally equal and of equal worth. Any social or political rule or institution must be judged according to whether it is consistent with that basic egalitarian premise. If a law does not treat all human beings as equal and provide everyone with an opportunity to flourish with dignity, then it is an unjust law and should be ignored.

P: But if a law has been produced by the representatives of a democratic society, Diogenes, surely it must be obeyed?

D: A law is not 'just' merely because it has been produced by a democratic society, Plato. The mob can be the mother of tyrants. We know all too well many examples of unjust laws being produced by democracies, so we cannot mindlessly assume all laws are just, for we know they are not. Thus the ultimate authority can only be one's own critical conscience. Would you not agree, Plato, that one should act in accordance with one's conscience?

P: Necessarily, Diogenes, for one's conscience, informed by reason and evidence, is the only moral compass we have.

D: Then you must also accept that if a democracy produces an unjust law, then a just man or woman has no obligation to respect such a law.

P: I do accept that, Diogenes. Justice could not require us to obey unjust laws.

D: Moreover, if a law is unjust it would seem that justice would require a person to actively defy it, for surely it is unjust to sit quietly and do nothing in an unjust situation, is it not?

P: Inaction is an act, Diogenes, for which one must be held responsible. So yes, one must not acquiesce in the face of an unjust law or an unjust system, but must actively oppose such things.

D: You are sounding like a radical, Plato.

P: Well, you have merely cleared some of obstacles in the way of clear thinking, Diogenes. If evidence, ethical reflection, and logic all demand a radical position, radical one must be. It is odd, however, that a position should be called 'radical' despite the forces of reason and evidence being on one's side.

D: Such is the state of things, Plato. The consequence is that one must not conform unthinkingly to the laws, customs, and conventions of our times but must evaluate them against the higher authority of one's critical conscience. This is why I am not a citizen of any city or state, Plato. I am a citizen of the cosmos.

P: Perhaps you are, Diogenes. But what exactly do you mean by that?

D: Quite simply, I am a citizen of the cosmos because my sense of duty and love does not start or stop at the borders of city-states or of our Empire but expands to the entire community of life. Moral progress, to my mind, is about expanding our arms of compassion to embrace ever more people and things, rather than only caring for ourselves and our inner circle of family and friends. An enlightened creature will even love the soil beneath his or her feet, and thus tread lightly.

P: An intriguing perspective, I have to say. But tell me, Diogenes, you have talked much of opposition and defiance. What of your positive vision? What does your ideal Republic look like?

D: I would be delighted to share my thoughts, and there is only one place to start: any just Republic, Plato, must begin by paying due regard to Nature, for Nature is the foundation of everything, including our economy.

P: Please elaborate, Diogenes.

D: Everything we eat and drink; everything we use to build our houses, warm our rooms, or light our lanterns; every fibre that clothes our bodies – all this and so much more comes from Nature. So it would follow that we must not degrade Nature, because if Nature is not healthy, our economy cannot be healthy. Would you agree?

P: That is so obvious that I am surprised it needs to be stated.

D: Obvious though it is, Plato, such truths must be stated in a world that seeks to defy them. A just Republic must show respect to Gaia and live within her limits.

P: None could deny that, Diogenes, for else Gaia would take her revenge upon us! The worry is that we need her, but she doesn't need us.

D: Indeed. Now, having accepted that a just economy must respect the limits of Gaia, several things follow. First of all, it implies that our culture must not celebrate material luxury and extravagance as a path to prosperity, because if we all pursued that path, undoubtedly we would exceed the limits of Gaia.

P: Clearly that is so. I am sure, for example, if Epicurus chopped down every tree or plant in his thriving garden in order to sell them at the marketplace, he would think he was rich for a short time… and then feel very poor and foolish when he discovered he had destroyed his own livelihood. Similarly for the national or global scale: if everyone lived affluently, Gaia would surely collapse under the weight of our vain accumulations.

D: Yes. And a way of life that cannot be universalised to all humanity is illegitimate, is it not?

P: One could not argue otherwise without believing oneself superior to and more deserving than others.

D: Yes, and we have already agreed that a just Republic assumes all human beings are inherently equal from a moral perspective, haven't we?

P: We have.

D: It follows that a just Republic must be founded upon a material culture that respects the natural limits of Gaia. This means cultivating an ethics of moderation, frugality, and sufficiency, for without a sense of 'enough' a citizenry would forever pursue 'more', and that would logically lead to the consumption and production of 'too much', would it not?

P: It would, Diogenes, necessarily. But doesn't material sufficiency imply hardship and sacrifice? Many people assume the good life consists primarily in material riches. The simple life doesn't seem so attractive.

D: We have established that if everyone pursues ever increasing material wealth as the path to prosperity, Gaia will collapse and we will all perish; none shall prosper. So the good life cannot consist in material riches. On the contrary, universal prosperity – long term and short term – lies only in enlightened material restraint.

P: I can accept that forever pursuing more will lead to the ruin of all but you have yet to explain why material sufficiency is the foundation of a good life, here and now.

D: Are there not an infinite variety of rich, meaningful, and fulfilling lives that are consistent with living a simple life based on material sufficiency?

P: Yes, Diogenes, the richness of simplicity knows no bounds, because the good things in life are free – although, alas, few people have the wisdom to see this.

D: Yes, human blindness in this regard is the greatest failing of our species, Plato. Closing the door of materialism in favour of a life of simplicity does not even limit our freedom really, because there are still infinite doors through which we could walk. We will see a great leap forward in the story of civilisation the moment we turn away from our materialistic pursuits and turn to the realm of the spirit to satisfy our hunger for infinity.

P: I dream of that day, Diogenes. May I have some more lentils?

Diogenes obliges.

D: Just as a materialistic culture is inconsistent with the limits of Gaia, so too is an economy that seeks to expand limitlessly, am I right?

P: That is but the other side of the same coin, Diogenes. You are merely suggesting that an economy ought to be shaped in accordance with the laws of nature, which is hardly profound. An economy cannot expand limitlessly on a finite planet; only idiots with lentils for brains would think otherwise.

D: Yes, the entire community of life has a right to flourish within the natural limits of Gaia. But since there are so many of us – which is a large part of the problem we must solve! – this means that we must be mindful of our rage to consume and procreate, for else we will undermine the foundations of our existence and the existence of other species.

P: When I look at our rivers, forests, and soils, Diogenes, it would seem that we are already undermining the foundations of life.

D: Yes, we are, Plato – brutally and with disgraceful ignorance. The consequence is that our affluent culture cannot merely give up the pursuit of 'more'. Instead, those who are living materialistic lives must actually learn to produce and consume a great deal less, not only for their own sake but also for the sake of people and planet more generally. There is no other way to avoid catastrophe.

P: Your reasoning is robust, Diogenes, but what of those people who live in genuine destitution? Don't they have a right to more?

D: Of course they do, Plato. Everyone has the right to 'enough' – the basic material conditions for freedom and wellbeing. So if those conditions are not met, it is our collective duty to resolve that injustice in due acknowledgement of the equal moral worth of all human beings. Good citizens are born neither of hunger nor excess.

P: But if our economies have already pushed beyond the safe limits, does that not mean that economic expansion to provide for the destitute will merely degrade the natural world even further? Here we face a paradox: it would seem we must grow our economies for the sake of social justice but contract our economies for the sake of nature.

D: Why, Plato, there is a simple and elegant solution to your paradox: not by baking a larger and larger economic pie but by slicing it differently! There is enough in this world for everyone if we all take enough, but there can never be enough for all if some take too much. A just Republic would set boundaries around accumulation to ensure that there was neither poverty nor extravagance.

P: You are going to make enemies of the rich saying things like that, Diogenes. These days sharing is considered subversive.

D: The rich don't need me to be their enemy, Plato, for they are enemies enough to themselves. You just need to look at them to see they are rotten inside, which is perhaps why they need such nice clothes. They try to hide their internal decay.

P: The revolution will begin, perhaps, when more people awaken to the false example of the rich and show the courage to seek alternative ways to flourish.

D: Yes, that is the spark that can ignite the fire. But while the revolution needed must begin with people rejecting greed and avarice and embracing humble lives of voluntary simplicity, personal action alone is far from enough. We must also come together as self-governing communities to build new forms of social and economic life that promote and encourage voluntary simplicity, ensure fair distribution, and show due respect for nature. Fortunately, from a practical perspective, this can be done with relative ease, if only we decide that this is what we want.

P: Yes, but I do not think we can rely on our politicians to assist much here, for they seem most concerned with the advancement of their own power and position, not the betterment of the Republic or maintaining the integrity of Gaia.

D: Indeed. Empire will fight for existence all the way down. Thus we must build the new world ourselves, here and now. The market system of Empire is a machine, broken beyond repair, that locks people into sad, degenerate lives; locks merchants into vile competition in order to produce the most trinkets; and locks states into violent wars that are required to maintain the existing form of civilisation that is destroying its natural foundations. This machine cannot be fixed, so together, we must turn it inside out, by finding cracks in it and leveraging change by living inspired alternatives in collective opposition and renewal. If enough of us start living simply and building the new world together in that spirit, the machine will become obsolete.

P: Diogenes, you have seen deeply into the state of things. Where most people see material riches as the path to progress, you have demonstrated that affluence is a false god that will merely lead to the ruin of all. There are many matters of detail that could go one way or the other, but if a community were to begin with the principles you outline, it could not go too far astray.

D: I am heartened to hear you say that, Plato. There is one thing I should add. The foundation of every flourishing society lies in the education of its youth. After all, how can a government expect to function, no matter how well crafted its laws or customs, if most of its citizens live greedy and degenerate lives?

P: I cannot imagine how it could function, Diogenes, so I agree that the great transformation, nay, the revolution, must begin with education, broadly conceived. We must learn or relearn how to live well and be free within the limits of Gaia. It is the defining challenge of our times.

D: Do you now accept, Plato, that the only just Republic is a self-governing, egalitarian society based on a culture and economy of 'simple living'?

P: Yes, Diogenes, your logic has been inescapable.

D: You must also accept, then, that the current laws of our government are grossly unjust, because those laws fundamentally contradict this vision of a simple living utopia.

P: There is no other way to see things.

D: On that basis, Plato, a just person such as yourself must feel duty-bound to live in opposition to such laws, and spend one's time and resources building a new world that better accords with the vision and values we have just been discussing.

P: Certainly, Diogenes. And now I must bid you farewell, because before I stand before my students today and hope to teach them anything worthwhile about politics, I must make some fundamental revisions to my lecture. You have made a revolutionary of me, Diogenes.

D: I have merely shown you the light in a dark world.

ACT IV

THE NERVOUS OLIGARCHS

With the Emperor out of the city on official business, the oligarchs of the Empire gather to discuss the problem of Diogenes and their dissatisfaction with the Emperor's failure to respond to his subversive teachings. Servants lay an extravagant banquet of exotic foods and fine wines and the oligarchs feast like pigs. Eventually, the plump man at the head of the table taps his goblet with a fork and begins to speak.

First Oligarch [O1]: Noble and esteemed gentlemen, may I have your attention. It is probably time that we get down to business, for time is a-wasting – and we all know time is money and that money is of paramount importance.

Everyone at the table laughs, knowing full well the speaker is not jesting.

O1: We are here, as you know, to discuss the problem of Diogenes and his so-called 'doctrine of simplicity', such that it is. This man is a joke, although he is no longer a laughing matter, for his ideas are quickly spreading from person to person, as if by means invisible. He is corrupting our fine polity and has even infected our impressionable young Emperor with his dog philosophy. Plato, no less, has started teaching Diogenes' *Republic* instead of his own at the

Academy! I, for one, will not stand for it. We must act immediately to rid ourselves of this wretched menace, for the dog threatens the natural order and our place at the top.

Others: Hear, hear.

O1: The question, then, is what is to be done? Let us first consider the nature of our problem.

Second Oligarch [O2]: Allow me to begin by sharing my personal take on the subject. Last week I was at a banquet and for some reason I cannot comprehend our host had invited Diogenes to dine with us – to entertain his guests with that clown of a man, one can only assume. In any case, midway through the meal one hears Diogenes coughing madly and he proceeds to get up and run around the room like a headless chook. After a time the dog stops next to our host and spits in his face! Would you believe such a thing! After much commotion it was demanded that Diogenes explain his conduct.

O1: And what did he have to say for himself?

O2: He claimed that because the room was so lavishly furnished with expensive carpets and sumptuous cushions he couldn't find anywhere suitable to displace the phlegm in his throat, and so he had to settle for what he claimed was the meanest and dirtiest place in the room. It was an outrage, I tell you, a scandal, a humiliation, not only to our host but also to our very way of life. Naturally, Diogenes was promptly thrown back on the streets with the other dogs.

O1: It is where he belongs!

Others: Hear, hear.

O2: He has no place in civilised society!

Others: Hear, hear.

Third Oligarch [O3]: Well, my friends, if you think that is scandalous, listen to this. Three nights ago I, too, was at a banquet where Diogenes was also invited. He seems very keen to enjoy other people's wine and shamelessly admits that it is his favourite variety. He should take a lesson from us, I say, who would never take advantage of public wealth. During the meal the conversation turned to philosophy and we found ourselves having to endure the dog evangelising about the so-called riches of poverty. I can't say I could fault the logic of his reasoning, but so odious were his conclusions that everyone at the table agreed that they had to be false. Given that I was the wealthiest man at the table I found his perspectives particularly offensive, so in the hope of changing the subject I mockingly threw the bones on my plate to Diogenes, as one would throw bones to a dog, and encouraged him to feast away under the table where he belonged.

O2: Tell us, what happened next?

O3: You will not believe it but I swear it happened. After gnawing gratefully on the bones for a few minutes, removing every thread of flesh from them, he crawled under the table, where I hoped he would at last sit quietly for once. But the next thing I knew the dog had lifted his leg and was pissing on me. I jest not! It was simply revolting!

O1: The man is insane!

O3: If the others had not intervened I swear that I would have killed Diogenes right there and then. Fortunately for the dog our host did not want blood on his new marble floor, so out of respect for his possessions I maintained my composure. Of course, Diogenes was again thrown out on the streets. I can't imagine he'll be invited to any more dinner parties after behaviour like that.

O2: May he die of hunger in his filthy kennel!

Others: Hear, hear.

Fourth Oligarch [O4]: My experience has not been quite so obscene but it is equally insulting, perhaps even to the point of treason. Some time ago I mobilised our armies at Alexander's request, for the purposes of expanding our noble Empire. As I did so I am told that Diogenes began rolling his tub up and down the hill on the promenade, mimicking Sisyphus no doubt. When asked what he was doing, he sniped that he wanted to look as busy as the rest of us. One can only assume he does not understand the necessity and justice of our wars. Honestly, how else does he expect our Empire to obtain its riches and maintain our way of life if not through eternal war?

O2: I think this is precisely where the uncivilised dog is at his most seditious: he simply does not believe in our civilisation or the values upon which it is based. Both in his speech and his action, he is inciting discontent with our cherished customs and conventions, undermining the established order and everything we hold dear. There is a collective rumbling in our world today and I know that it is he who is banging the drum of rebellion. Every day we permit him to live, I tell you, he will continue to stoke the embers of revolution and flare people's utopian ambitions. His doctrine of simplicity is like oxygen, it seems, and I fear that the embers are about to ignite and turn our Empire into ashes. This is not an indulgence I am prepared to make for a dog!

Others: Hear, hear.

O1: You have, I believe, touched the core of the matter. His doctrine of simplicity implies nothing less than a revolutionary agenda. Thus, for the sake of our noble Empire this menace must be brought to justice – our justice, not his. Just imagine, after all, if more people escaped the market, following the dog's lead, only to find contentment in the simple life. What would happen to all the hard-working merchants selling trinkets to the masses? Their businesses would come to an end, no doubt. And then what?

O2: I will tell you what would happen: our economy would collapse! And the suffering that this would cause would be unbearable, not only for us, but also for all those who rely on the economy, especially the poor. Verily, we must bring an end to Diogenes for the sake of the poor and protect them from his dangerous, destabilising nonsense.

O3: Yes, we must maintain the existing system for the sake of the poor.

Others: Hear, hear.

Q1 barks orders at the servants to bring more wine.

O4: For so long our control over culture has been remarkably effective, minimising the extent to which ideas such as simplicity, moderation, and love of nature, could contaminate the citizenry. But somehow we are losing control of the collective imagination. I worry that the common people are beginning to believe that other worlds are possible.

O1: Yes, Diogenes is providing an example of an alternative way of life, showing that, by minimising the need for material riches, one is liberated from the labour otherwise required to get those riches. I ask you all: who is supposed to grow our food, build and clean our houses, make our trinkets, and serve our tables, if people discover that by living in accordance with nature they do not need to labour for superfluous things?

O3: Precisely. How is our economy supposed to function if people are free to provide for themselves? Who would serve us? By all accounts the dog has written a book describing a world in which everyone lives simply, freely, and happily, undifferentiated by class. What nonsense! What place is there for us in such a world?

O2: None at all.

The servants, who had been listening to all this, suddenly leave the room without permission and do not return. There is a long silence as the oligarchs look nervously at each other.

O1: Gentlemen, it seems clear enough that we are in unanimous agreement about the grave threat that Diogenes and his teachings represent. We must act quickly and decisively while our Emperor is away on official business, to avoid having to seek his approval, which, I suspect, would not be forthcoming.

Others: Hear, hear.

O1: We are all merciful men, there is no doubt about that, but in this instance we must act with an iron fist, for the sake of maintaining order and justice. It is with some regret, therefore, that I propose that we confiscate and destroy the dog's literature – every seditious page of it – and further, that we issue a warrant for the arrest of Diogenes and proceed to execution at the earliest convenience. We would not want our plans thwarted by a naïve Emperor who does not know what is good for him.

Others: Hear, hear.

O3: Gentlemen, might I propose that we engage my daughter to carry out the confiscation of the dog's literature? We need someone we can trust completely and I can vouch for her ability. Furthermore, she has no time for the dog or his philosophy.

O1: I was going to propose her myself. Are there any objections?

None at the table object.

O3: Very well, I shall speak with her this very evening and insist that the task be completed by the week's end.

O1: Excellent.

O2: Allow me to suggest one thing further, my esteemed friends, for no doubt I am merely speaking out loud what we are all thinking. Should we not take care of our Emperor the same day we take care of Diogenes? If you will excuse the paradox, sometimes only sedition can quash the seditious.

O1: Your words are difficult but necessary, and your bravery for raising this issue is to be commended. For the sake of our Empire, I, for one, can see no alternative to your additional proposal.

O4: Nor I.

O3: Nor I.

O2: If it would please you all, then, I would be happy to make plans for Iollas to assist us with this official business. Perhaps we could gift Alexander a 'special' drink?

There is much nodding of heads.

O1: Are we agreed, then?

Others: Hear, hear.

O1: Thus let it be done.

O2: To the glory of Empire!

Others: Hear, hear.

The oligarchs raise their goblets and proudly toast to their sedition.

ACT V

THE RENEGADE

The confiscation of Diogenes' books by the military was carried out with ruthless efficiency and breathtaking speed. It was followed up by a Public Decree stating that any person caught with any of Diogenes' writings, or any person found knowing of the existence of a copy and not reporting it, would be guilty of high treason and summarily executed. The citizenry was in a state of terror and duly obliged, not wanting to die for a philosopher. Nevertheless, the oligarch's daughter who had been tasked with coordinating this colossal act of state censorship, and who had done so without question, was beginning to have harrowing doubts about the legitimacy of the entire endeavour. She alone had access to the tower in which all copies of Diogenes' works had been collected, and owing to some deep, irrepressible urge found herself one evening secretly reading the very books she had been ordered to destroy. All night she read with unprecedented focus and attention, every page striking her mind, heart, and soul with the force of deep truth, shattering the illusions of her false sense of reality and infecting her with that strange form of insanity that flows only from enlightenment. As the sun began to creep over the horizon, she left the tower, locked the heavy door, and in a hooded cloak made her way through the back roads towards Diogenes' tub, not knowing exactly why or to what end.

She found Diogenes already awake, humming to himself as he gathered berries from the roadside near his tub.

The Renegade [R]: It looks like you are gathering a worthy meal there, stranger.

Diogenes glances up to see the hooded visitor standing near his tub, her face obscured. He continues to forage.

Diogenes [D]: A dog eats what he can find, beg, or steal, and is content with that, whether it is worthy or not. Fine tastes serve only to make slaves of people, you know? Berries or weeds, it's all the same to me. I sometimes wonder whether I could not survive on sunlight alone.

Diogenes sits down on a patch of grass, throws a couple of berries in his mouth and turns to examine his mysterious visitor. There is a short silence.

R: I presume you have heard, Diogenes, that your books have been confiscated by the state and that there is a warrant out for your arrest. You must have been out wandering these last few days, for otherwise I am sure you would have already been imprisoned.

D: Of what use is a philosopher who doesn't hurt anybody's feelings?

R: That may be so, Diogenes, but aren't you angry that your works are being censored? Don't you fear for your wellbeing? For the wellbeing of Truth?

D: If I spent my time worrying about what stupid things the people of this world were doing or saying I'd be in a terrible condition, I can tell you that. I would probably explode, literally, with a mixture of pity and rage. I change the things I can and otherwise love the fate that is bestowed upon me. *Amor fati*. It's quite simple really. I regret nothing.

R: Your courage is admirable, Diogenes, both in word and in deed, to the point of recklessness, one might say. In fact, that is partly why I am here. I have been reading your books and they have made quite an impression on me. They have shaken me awake, so to speak, and given my life a new sense of meaning and purpose. But more importantly, I feel they could spark a revolution in consciousness in our city, our nation, nay, even our civilisation, so it disturbs me that your words may soon be lost to the world.

D: I don't know why you or anyone feels the need to read my books, which I write primarily for the clarification of my own thoughts. To learn my lessons it would serve you better just to come and watch me live – or better yet, to come and join me! If people want figs they wouldn't be satisfied with painted ones, I presume? But people take no notice of the practice of virtue and study only those who write about it.

R: Admittedly, I have arrived late to this scene of simplicity, Diogenes, but I am here now as a result of your books and am grateful to you for having drawn me to the light. Nevertheless, so long was I in darkness that today my eyes are still adjusting to the brightness of this new perspective, and I find myself in many ways deeply troubled and confused. Humbly, I have come to seek your counsel in the hope that you might be able to resolve some of my inner discord.

Curious, Diogenes stands up and walks towards the hooded stranger. Near his tub he picks up his burning lantern and holds it up to her face as if to assess her character. After a time he slowly nods his head.

D: You seem to be a genuine seeker, so perhaps you're not here to waste my time, after all. What troubles could a person face that would drive them to seek the counsel of a dog? You must be disturbed, indeed.

There is a silence while the visitor gathers her thoughts.

R: Diogenes, allow me, if you will, to provide a little background to my life, purely to give my troubles some context.

D: Context is everything, says Heraclitus, and yet context is ever changing. Please share what you think is necessary for our discussion to bear fruit.

R: Well, I grew up in this city of Athens, you see, living a life of not inconsiderable privilege. My parents, while not rich compared to some, are very comfortable and well respected in the community, and by any standard it could be said I was raised in conditions of affluence. I am well educated, healthy, and obedient – a model citizen you could say. In a certain sense, I would even say that I have lived a happy life, although that is a question to which I should like to return. But for now just let me make clear that the world has been kind to me and that, until very recently, I had always thought that I was entitled to this good fortune, that I deserved it. After all, everyone whom I have ever associated with explicitly or implicitly told me that I deserved it, and perhaps I even returned to them this same courtesy as an act of mutual self-congratulation.

D: So the world has been kind to you and given you more than you could possibly need. Tell me, why has this only now become a thorn in your side?

R: Well, Diogenes, to begin with, I have only recently come to see that the privileges of my life and my rank in society are essentially arbitrary – bestowed upon me without good cause.

D: Ha! I worry about the state of your intellect if it took you this long to see such a self-evident truth. And just now you were telling me you were well educated! Such is the state of things, I suppose.

R: I am embarrassed by my blindness, Diogenes.

D: Blushing is the colour of virtue, so at least you have that.

R: My face has never been redder than it is today, Diogenes, I assure you. Yes, I have worked hard in my life, not without a certain kind of honour, but I am sure you will point out that so does the devil work hard. If only you knew the nature of some of my deeds, it would make you sick.

D: I have lived with humanity for a long time, stranger. Believe me, my gut is robust.

R: No doubt that is true. What I know for myself is that the most significant things that have determined my position on the ladder of life are really not owing to my efforts or self-worth at all, but instead are mostly the result of a natural lottery conducted within an unjust system, and per chance I just happened to be one of the few winners. Just as easily I could have been born in the most miserable poverty, with the most debilitating diseases, to parents who were violent and uncaring, and so on. And then what might I have become? I hate to think.

D: Perhaps you feel that in different conditions you might have been capable of a life of crime and violence yourself?

R: Precisely, Diogenes, although my realisation is more disturbing still. I have come to see that part of the reason so many are downtrodden in this world is precisely because a few, such as myself, have acquired such vast proportions of nature's wealth. So, worse than knowing that I *could* have been capable of living a life of crime and violence myself, I now see that in fact I *have lived* a life of crime and violence, only surreptitiously. I was blind to this reality because the propertied class to which I belong tells itself relentlessly that our way of life is noble and just – and it is very easy to believe people when they insist that you are noble and just. Humans rarely question such commendations.

D: I can understand why your privilege is a cause of turmoil, stranger. Admittedly, I once knew such turmoil myself, for similar reasons.

R: It heartens me to hear that, Diogenes, in a strange sort of way. For it suggests there is hope for me yet. But then I look at how you are living and I become scared to the point of paralysis. My convictions weaken, and I find myself merely expounding values that I could not possibly live by, remaining part of the problems I would genuinely like to help solve. Do you understand my conflict, Diogenes? For all intents and purposes I am winning the rat race, you see! Perhaps a saint like you could give up the wealth, privilege, status, and security I have and follow the dogs, to run a different race, but I am a mere mortal. I know that my life is an unjustifiable sham but I cannot imagine giving it up. I haven't the courage.

D: If your life is a sham and you know this, but you do not give it up to live in accordance with your values, surely you have already given up on life and are merely pretending to live?

R: Your logic cuts me like a knife, Diogenes, to the bone! Be delicate with me, please, or you will only deepen my breakdown or make me turn away.

D: Other dogs bite only their enemies, whereas I also bite my friends in order to save them. Please interpret my words in that vein, delicate stranger. There comes a time in everyone's life when they must honestly face the question: how is one to live? Those who have virtue always in their mouths, and neglect it in practice, are like a harp that emits a sound pleasing to others, while itself is insensible of the music.

R: Yes, Diogenes, precisely! I want to hear the music of virtue! I want to live it, sincerely and deliberately! But at every turn my nature conspires against me. I am weak, or choose to be weak. It seems that I would prefer to suffer the guilt of my affluence than the uncertainty that would flow from giving it up.

D: There's nothing to be uncertain about should you give up affluence: you'd have to live like a poet!

Diogenes laughs.

R: I find it hard to laugh with you, Diogenes. This is a real burden in my life, and I'm sure there are countless others like me, who live in affluence but who don't believe their affluence is legitimate given its rotten foundations. We are legion, no doubt. We are everywhere – although few speak up, meaning that those who are asking these questions often feel isolated and alone.

D: The fact that you were born into a position of wealth and privilege is not the problem, so spare yourself – and spare me – all your talk of guilt. It quickly gets tiresome. After all, you had no choice about where you were born! We are thrown into an existence without being consulted. But you do have choice about what you are going to *do* with your wealth and privilege. That is something worth taking very seriously and raises more interesting questions. Are you going to invest your energies and resources into building a world where everyone can flourish? Or are you just going to sit on nice furniture and eat exotic food like a silly git? There is much more to life than that, I assure you.

R: I know there is more to life, Diogenes, there must be more, because I have tasted the emptiness of affluence. The bittersweet pleasures of trinkets, such that they are, are nice enough, but they are everywhere tinged and tarnished with an existential sadness that knows no specific loss. You can see this sadness in the dead eyes of people whose greatest concern is their trinkets. I fear this spiritual malaise has come to define our times – although I suspect I don't need to convince you of that.

D: No, you do not. Trinkets and trifles cannot satisfy the universal human desire for meaning, for we all crave a deeper satisfaction that cannot be found in the marketplace. The tragedy is that when people don't find fulfilment in the marketplace, they think it is because they haven't spent enough money! Arrgh! What I do not understand, however, is why you don't do something about these issues? Why don't you swim against the tide of culture?

R: This is where it gets complicated, Diogenes, so I'll do my best to explain myself. It seems to me that human beings are not unlike authors of a book, and we are each tasked with writing our own story, so to speak. We must do our best to be coherent authors.

D: The analogy has much to commend it. But what's your point?

R: Yes, well, the thing is, as time goes on, certain expectations are formed about the nature of the story being written – both by the author and society. After all, when you are half way through a book, you want and expect your story to remain coherent, and that means shaping everything you do in forthcoming chapters of life in a way that fits with what has already been done. This points to a major problem for me, I think, and others like me – perhaps even for our civilisation at large. We have been telling a story about ourselves for so long that we find it hard to imagine telling a fundamentally new story. So when you say, 'just swim against the tide', I think you make light of the challenge somehow. There are forces at play here that are not insignificant.

D: So – let me get it straight – even when human beings know they should be telling a new story, they persevere with the old story, like unimaginative cowards, because they want to remain *coherent*. I'm not sure what you are wanting from me. I can only offer my indignation.

R: Perhaps we are unimaginative cowards, Diogenes, but don't you see the difficulty of the situation? My friends, family, lovers, and associates, all expect me to conform more or less to the status quo, to be the person I have always been, just as I expect the same of them, unthinkingly. We lock ourselves into business as usual – and guess what we get?

D: Business as usual.

R: Precisely. To do otherwise – to reject the affluence and create a new life, a new identity – this would require taking the story of my life in a totally new direction, as if a new author had taken over my book and decided to change the plot, the themes, the characters, and the ending. It would be incoherent, I say! People would think I was mad! My identity would be in tatters. I wouldn't know who I was, nor would others... and so I stay the same.

D: Look, life itself will cast your narrative into incoherent directions no matter what, which is to say, your life will *be* incoherent, whether you want it to be or not. So why not allow yourself the freedom to introduce that incoherence by choice rather than by accident? In the end, it will amount to the same thing, except in the first instance you are the product of history, and in the second case, you are its author.

R [pause]: Perhaps you are right, Diogenes. But beyond this internal bind, everyone faces the external challenge too. We do not live in a neutral world, where all ways of living are given equal opportunity to flourish. A neutral world in that regard is impossible. Every society, every economy, every government, creates structures that promote certain ways of living and inhibit other ways of living. We are currently living in a world that promotes materialistic ways of living and inhibits the simpler ways that you practise. I might dream of a world that encourages simplicity of living, but, alas, find myself in a world that makes it almost impossible, despite your noble example. And thus I feel essentially locked into a way of life that I find deeply unsatisfying, destructive, and unjust, but do not know what can be done or where to direct my vital energies. I am lost and confused, without a compass to guide my festering discontent.

Diogenes yawns loudly.

D: Are you finished?

R: There is much more to say, of course, but for now perhaps I've said more than enough.

D: Indeed. I get the sense you are trying to solve your problems with methods that are unnecessarily complex. Do not expect black and white answers, rigid rules, and equations into which you can plug the facts of your life and be told how to live. Life is a blurry mess of ethical ambiguities. But there are some general principles that can provide some guidance.

R: Please, Diogenes, go on. You have my fullest attention.

D: Be honest; be brave; be creative. The real challenge you face is not so much about *how* to live but *whether* to live. Once you have affirmed or reaffirmed life, the details will follow in due course. Are you prepared to say 'yes' to life?

R: I am, Diogenes – yes!

D: Let us, then, begin with honesty. We must all do everything we can to *live the truth*, as we best understand it, however shocking or challenging it may be. You seem to have acquired an insight into the truth but hitherto have lacked the courage to live in accordance with it. This is the cause of your festering discontent, stranger, because knowing that you live unjustly yet continuing in your ways, your subconscious recognises you as a fraud no matter what you tell yourself or what others tell you about who you are. Do not try to escape the truth, because wherever you go, there truth will be, to expose you.

R: I think I understand, Diogenes.

D: I should hope so, for I have been perfectly clear. Now, having recognised that the affluence that defines your way of life is illegitimate and for the most part an arbitrary and oppressive privilege, you must then show the courage of your convictions. Be brave – be brave enough to be incoherent! Be brave enough to be sane in an insane world and thus appear mad! Create someone new! Be a pioneer! The world is full of cowards who would sooner conform to the ridiculous customs and conventions of polite society than speak up and live otherwise. Do not fear the laughter of asses, my friend, or else you will end up an ass. I would sooner have the respect of a small number of lions and owls – or merely maintain self-respect – than be esteemed by a herd of asses. Too often I see people frittering away their lives trying to impress the masses of asses.

R: You are making perfect sense, Diogenes, painful though it is to acknowledge. It would be devastating to get to the end of life only to discover that one spent it seeking the good opinion of fools.

D: Precisely. As I see things, for what it is worth, you might find it easy enough to be honest, and I suspect there is a brave pioneer within you desperately wanting to break free from the shackles of conventional living and to create new cultural paths into the future. So far, so good. What is less clear to me is whether you have the imagination to do so. You have written in life many chapters of a boring book, celebrating your arbitrary privileges and justifying your oppression. Can you now, at this late stage, change the story? Can you yet make the story interesting, creative, and beautiful? You talk of unhappiness and discontent: don't you see that you have this wondrous opportunity to reimagine your life beyond the marketplace and find unexpected delights in oppositional living? To live simply in a materialistic culture is not to give up on the promise of a meaningful life but to demand its fulfilment. Wake up, stranger, for time is passing. Claim your freedom, however heavy the burden. I believe in you. *Wake up!*

Suddenly a number of imperial guards enter the scene and point to Diogenes. The stranger quickly covers her face with her hood and scurries away before being identified.

Diogenes offers no resistance as he is arrested and taken away.

ACT VI

DIOGENES IN PRISON

Diogenes sits in a dank prison cell, alone but not lonely. He has been given no explanation for his incarceration other than the vague charges of 'corrupting the polity' and 'undermining the natural order', both of which are punishable by death. It also has been conveyed to Diogenes that for reasons of efficiency the authorities have chosen to bypass his trial and proceed straight to the sentence, which will be carried out imminently. To make an example of him, Diogenes is to be burnt at the stake, with his books fuelling the fire. While he awaits his execution, his young friend, Philiscus, from the marketplace, is granted permission to visit. A guard leads the boy through the descending stairwell to Diogenes' cell and then leaves the two friends alone to converse through iron bars.

Boy [B]: I cannot wish you a good morning, Diogenes, because it is a horrible morning, seeing a heavenly dog, born of Zeus, locked up like this and knowing what lies ahead. No dog should be in a cage. But it is good to see you again.

The boy embraces Diogenes through the bars.

Diogenes [D]: I have never been so well or so regularly fed, my friend, so please do not worry about me. You know by now, I hope, that it is not events that can hurt a person; only the ignorant interpretation of events can do that. So rather than despair at my situation, I have chosen, naturally, to turn this apparent crisis into an opportunity to do some serious philosophising, free from the petty distractions of civilisation. It is a bit dark down here, I have to say, but otherwise it's a remarkably pleasant place to do some inner work. One's inner work is never done, you know.

B: Goodness, Diogenes, don't you think that at this stage in life you should take some rest?

D: What! If I were running in the stadium, ought I to slacken my pace when approaching the finish line? Ought I not rather put on speed? Life is to be lived to the end, boy, remember that, and certainly don't expect me of all people to fade away. I wish to devour myself alive until there is nothing left of me.

B: But don't you fear death, Diogenes?

D: Why, no, not in the slightest. After all, when it arrives, I'll be gone!

Diogenes laughs. The boy does not.

B: I hadn't thought of it that way, Diogenes. Even through these iron bars you continue to refine and expand my perspectives on life. In fact ... *[the boy pauses]* ... I have to confess that my reasons for visiting today are partly self-serving. You see, in recent days I have been somewhat preoccupied with a set of issues that have begun to eat me up inside, and I was hoping that perhaps you might be able to shed some light on the matters, as is your way.

D: Let me just check my schedule. *[Diogenes pretends to flick through pages of a notebook.]* It looks like I'm free... despite being in here.

The boy permits himself a wry smile.

B: You truly are imperturbable, Diogenes.

D: It is an acquired skill, young brother, an acquired skill. Tell me, what is on your mind? This old dog will help if he can.

B: Well, Diogenes, I hardly know where to begin. In recent months, through exposure to your life and ideas, I have come to see that life need not be a curse but can be a blessing, if people would only give up their vain pursuits and embrace a humble life of material simplicity, where true contentment lies. I have come to understand, through lived experience, that such a simple existence in and of itself is a sublime gift to be cherished, revered, and celebrated, and that human beings could easily flourish together in harmony with nature and each other if only we made wise decisions, decisions that are within our power to make.

D: You speak the truth, young brother, and I have nothing to add.

B: Surely, I say to myself, if we have made this horrid, destructive civilisation then we can also unmake it and build something better, freer, and more humane. Are we not free, despite our chains?

D: Behold, we are living proof of that, boy!

B: Perhaps we are. This belief in the possibility of change gives me grounded hope, Diogenes; it is the dream I have when I am awake. Another world is possible, I am sure of it. But just as the clarity of my vision for a new Republic has become ever more refined and coherent under your tutelage,

I have also gained deeper insight into the forces that be, both inside ourselves and out there, which sweep our civilisation along in its current form, with the momentum of one thousand tides.

D: What are you trying to say, my friend?

B: What I am trying to say, Diogenes, is that I have come to believe with unshakable conviction that human society could be beautiful, a true work of art, but at the same time I have lost all confidence that it ever will be beautiful. I need to find a way to resolve or learn to live with this paradox or contradiction – if that is even possible – for fear that it will otherwise drive me to despair. Even now, as I share these words, a sickness is forming in the depths of my being, for I worry that even you cannot untie this knot in my gut.

D: That may be, young brother, but let us not get ahead of ourselves. Often the problems and paradoxes of the world do not so much need to be resolved as dissolved, for when a paradox is properly perceived it disappears, does it not?

B: I believe so, Diogenes.

D: Well, then, do not despair just yet! In any case, if a time comes when despair in fact seems inescapable – and it may be inescapable for a thinking creature like yourself in an age such as this – then be aware that despair can often bear fruit in surprising ways, provided it is mindfully digested.

B: Please explain what you mean, Diogenes.

D: Sometimes we need to embrace the full range of dark emotions to fully understand the times we live in. So don't be too quick to dismiss despair as merely a weight that must drag you down. She can also help you rise. She has been a friend to me at times, I can promise you that, enriching my life just as the darker shades enrich a painting. The important thing is not to let the dark emotions dominate or take over.

B: I think I follow, Diogenes.

D: It may be that your inner challenges cannot be resolved by finding ways to avoid the despair of which you speak. In fact, perhaps you should not try so hard to move away from the darkness. I would counsel you instead to move toward the darkness unflinchingly and throw yourself into the abyss at once. Your feelings are natural. Do not repress them or they will simply re-emerge in some even less digestible form.

B: Your words resonate with me, Diogenes, but they are hardly comforting. Having thrown myself into the abyss, what then?

D: Why, simply let your eyes adjust to the darkness – and then make yourself at home, like I have done here in this cell. At that point, thank despair for her company and kindly ask her to leave.

B: But what if she doesn't leave? That's my worry! What if letting my eyes adjust to the darkness just means I am left seeing too much, too clearly, too deeply? What if at that point the death of our civilisation seems utterly inevitable, great suffering imminent, and that any efforts to change things appear futile? I'm not sure I could live in that condition, Diogenes.

D: Death is a part of life, is it not?

B: Surely it is, Diogenes.

D: Well, embrace that – work with it rather than against it – for it is nature's way. If, for example, you were master of an old dog, and that dog became sick near the end of its life, would you do everything in your power to extend the dog's life, no matter how much pain it was in? Or would there come a time when you might instead comfort the dog as it passed on, rather than prolong the suffering by delaying the inevitable?

B: If everything must die, Diogenes, then there seems little point in extending the life of something unnecessarily, especially if that merely extends pain and suffering.

D: Indeed. And so, too, with our civilisation. It has been born, developed, matured (in a sense), and is now facing its deterioration, decline, and death – no doubt to be followed by the rebirth of something new, like a Phoenix that emerges from the ashes. The task is to negotiate this cycle wisely, however difficult it proves to be, and to ensure that the best parts of the human story survive to the next stage. It seems that too many of your hopes and expectations are hinged on saving our civilisation, fixing it, reforming it. But could your aims in this regard be fundamentally misconceived, however well intentioned they might be?

B: I am beginning to think they might be.

D: Just as the life of a dog should not be extended unnaturally, so too should we avoid extending the life of a dying civilisation beyond its natural term. It would be undignified to do so.

B: Are you saying, then, Diogenes, that I should reorientate my goals? That instead of dedicating my efforts to saving our civilisation, I should instead do what I can to help civilisation die with dignity?

D: I am not telling you what to do or what to think. I am just trying to loosen the knot.

B: Thank you, Diogenes, you might be having some positive effect. But I am still left wondering: why should we struggle for a new world if our chances of succeeding seem slim to non-existent?

D: Because if you do not struggle for a new world, young brother, something noble in your heart and spirit would be lost. It is as simple as that, and I think deep down you already know this. I certainly can't imagine you being satisfied spending the rest of your days, knowing what you know, reading the newspapers and gossiping about the latest trinkets in the marketplace.

B: Certainly, Diogenes, that wouldn't be much of a way to go. The burden I carry is preferable to boredom.

D: Yes, of course it is. In the end, we should not expect the promise of a fairy tale ending to inspire our efforts or to justify our rejection of an unjust world. The hour is dark and it may get darker yet, and still nothing can ensure that a new dawn will come. We should not, however, ask whether we are going to win the war, but merely for which causes should we be fighting. Thus our question should not be: will we succeed? Our question is simply: what is the right thing to do?

There is a pause in the conversation as the boy reflects.

B: Suppose I were to accept what you say, Diogenes – and as always you make a persuasive case. I'd still be unsure how to answer precisely the question you pose: what *is* the right thing to do? When everything seems too little, too late, every answer to your question seems futile. This paralyses me. The trinkets suddenly seem like tempting distractions.

D: Ah, but again, your language of futility suggests to me that you have locked yourself in a prison where winning the war is the only touchstone of success. Set yourself free, my friend! My point has been that we can still live nobly even if, as is likely, we are to lose the war. That is the challenge we must set ourselves.

B: Do go on, Diogenes.

D: Well, you seem to have erected a monster so large and terrifying that we could not possibly defeat it, and even if we could defeat it, success would lie solely in some distant future. But what if success lies not in defeating the beast in the future but in refusing to create the beast, here and now? Perhaps you need to conceive of the revolution as something happening already, happening now, as we speak, rather than as a future possibility when we all storm the castle. This revolution is already underway, and you can find nourishment in it, even if the revolution does not ultimately succeed. On our deathbeds, we will want to have lived a life in service to the cause.

There is another pause as they both peer aimlessly into space.

D: In any case, young brother, every generation must live its own revolution, so thinking of revolution as an 'event' that could either succeed or fail is something of a misuse of language. Every revolution is merely an unfolding in the flow of revolt that knows no end.

B: That all makes perfect sense, Diogenes. But if you agree that our chances of building the new world successfully are so slim, it would follow that a great deal of suffering lies ahead – is that not true?

D: I would not deny the likelihood of that.

B: So even if we do our best to facilitate a dignified death of our civilisation, there seems to be no avoiding the fact that in the process of civilisational descent there will be huge amounts of instability, uncertainty, and tragedy. I am still trying to get my head and heart around how to deal with that. Perhaps naively, I had hoped for a smoother transition.

D: There is no magic elixir I or anyone else could provide to ease the pain and suffering that must inevitably accompany a sick society in its final days. It is a burden we must all bear, in our own ways – even if it is grossly unjust that those who caused the sickness may not suffer as much as the innocent. And yet, if we cannot wholly avoid suffering, we must do everything in our power to make sure that the pain and suffering is meaningful, for there is nothing worse than meaningless suffering.

B: No doubt that is true.

D: Some suffering can be meaningful, however, some hardship, enriching, just as comfort and ease can sometimes be humiliating, debilitating, even oppressive. There is hardship and tragedy ahead, no doubt, my friend, but often it is during times of trial when shallow lives of bad faith become exposed and people see, all at once, that the world as it is, is not how the world has to be. 'Apocalypse' does not mean the end of the world so much as it means the end of the world *as we know it*. One way or another, the looming Apocalypse will be an unveiling, a revelation, a disclosure.

B: Are you saying that in times of great disruption people might actually find themselves living with greater freedom and meaning than they were when they were living comfortably but without purpose?

D: That is exactly my point. Let us aspire to be like autumn leaves, whose colours are brightest and most beautiful during their era of demise and death. My point is not to celebrate disruption, of course, but to make the best of it. So go forth and choose your Apocalypse, young brother, and lead the way turning the crises of our times into opportunities for civilisation renewal. Be adaptable and resilient in the turbulent times ahead as you pioneer a simpler way to live beyond the shameful materialism that defines our age. And if you fail, may you fail with dignity. Most of all, however, continue being kind, to yourself and others. The challenge is less about 'what is one to do?' and more about 'how is one to be?' Courage to us all.

Just then the two friends become aware of the sound of heavy boots slowly making their way down the stairwell. As they look at each other it dawns upon them that the guards are coming to take Diogenes away for his public execution. The boy speaks first, his voice noticeably distressed.

B: Diogenes, it seems the end is near. Thank you for being an honest friend to me, a kindred soul residing in a different body. I will forever endeavour to live by your example.

On saying that the boy reaches inside his cloak and draws forth a small knife. As a tear rolls down his cheek, he holds the knife out for Diogenes through the bars.

B: In case you need a friend, Diogenes. Don't let them see you suffer. End things on your own terms.

Diogenes smiles softly, shaking his head.

D: Thank you, my friend, but put that away. No man is hurt but by himself. You can be sure I'll end things on my own terms.

The boy hesitates, wondering whether to insist that the knife be accepted. But as the sound of the guards draws nearer he quickly returns the knife to where it had been hidden, for fear of being caught with it.

B: If it is not too distressing to contemplate, Diogenes, would you like to provide me with any instructions for how to deal with your body, you know, after...

D: Just make sure I am buried face down, my friend, for I'd like to be looking towards the skies when, in the goodness of time, the world is turned upside down.

Diogenes smiles with the sparkle of revolution in his eyes.

B: Goodbye, Diogenes.

D: Go well, Philiscus.

The guards burst through the door. In desperation the boy attempts to hold them back, crying out in anger and sadness while striking out with all the power he can muster. For a time he manages to stall the guards in the thin corridor, as they are reluctant to strike him back. Eventually, however, he is cast roughly to the side and left to watch on as the guards unlock the cell. But as the iron door swings open they are all left standing there in disbelief, seeing that Diogenes is already dead – it would seem from having held his breath.

◆ ◆ ◆

A public announcement is soon made that Diogenes died in prison. As the evening light fades the collected writings of Diogenes are set alight, casting dancing shadows over the walls and grand pillars of the city square. The crowd watches on as the blaze slowly reduces to embers, with a small choir being courageous enough to show their respects by singing the 'Hymn to Frugality'.

A hooded stranger walks past the boy and stealthily slips a book into his cloak with only a whisper of explanation:

R: Keep the flame alive.

OTHER BOOKS FROM THE SIMPLICITY INSTITUTE

Sufficiency Economy: Enough, for Everyone, Forever (2015)
Samuel Alexander

Prosperous Descent: Crisis as Opportunity in an Age of Limits
(2015) Samuel Alexander

Simple Living in History: Pioneers of the Deep Future (2014)
edited by Samuel Alexander and Amanda McLeod

*The Hidden Door: Mindful Sufficiency as an Alternative to
Extinction* (2013) Mark A. Burch

Entropia: Life beyond Industrial Civilisation (2013)
Samuel Alexander

FOR MORE INFORMATION, SEE THE SIMPLICITY INSTITUTE

www.simplicityinstitute.org

ABOUT THE AUTHOR

Dr Samuel Alexander is a part-time lecturer with the Office for Environmental Programs, University of Melbourne, Australia. He teaches a course called 'Consumerism and the Growth Economy: Interdisciplinary Perspectives' in the Master of Environment. He is also co-director of the Simplicity Institute (www.SimplicityInstitute.org) and co-developer of the 'simpler way' demonstration project, Wurruk'an (www.Wurrukan.org). He writes regularly at the Simplicity Collective and posts most of his academic essays at www.TheSufficiencyEconomy.com.

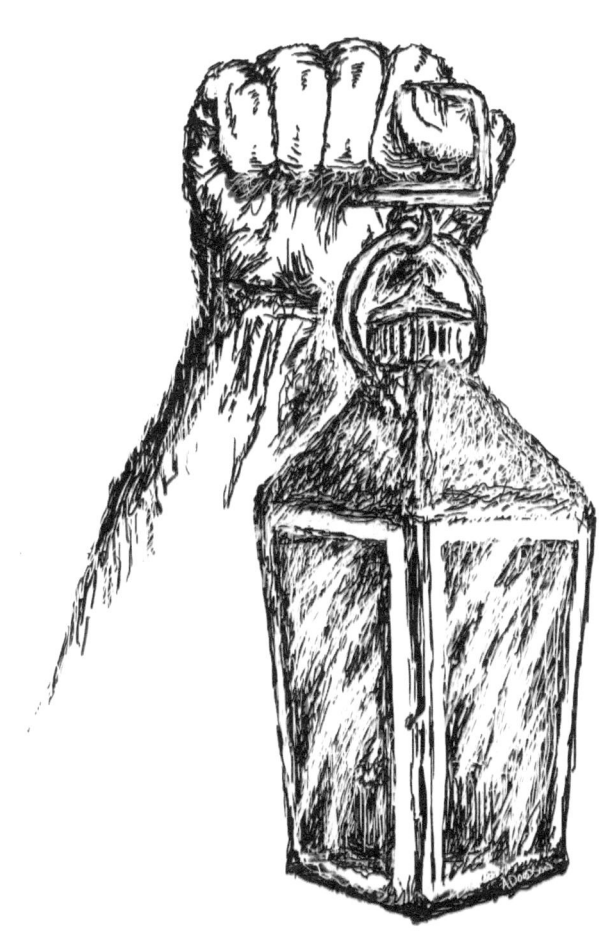

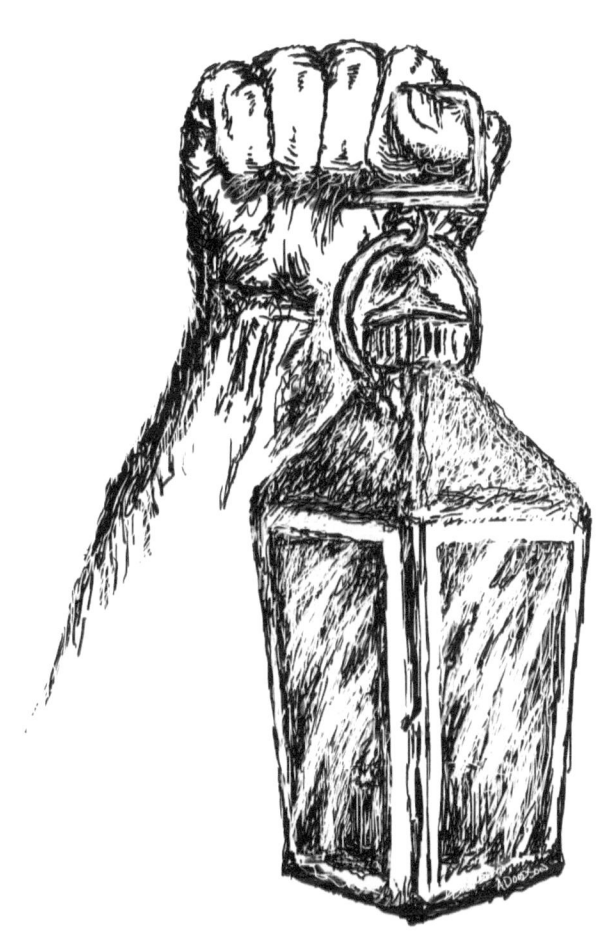

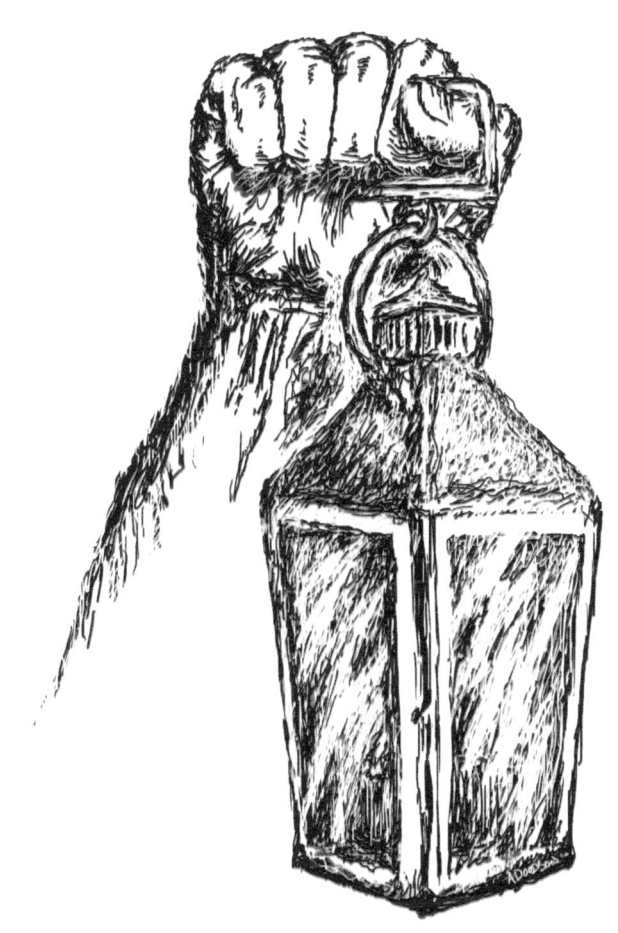

www.ingramcontent.com/pod-product-compliance
Lightning Source LLC
Chambersburg PA
CBHW020621300426
44113CB00007B/733